Embrace
Change

Hazelden Titles of Related Interest

Promise of a New Day
Worthy of Love

Also by Helene Lerner-Robbins

My Timing is Always Right
Stress Breakers

Embrace Change

Helene Lerner-Robbins

A Hazelden Book

HarperCollins*Publishers*

FIRST HARPERCOLLINS PAPERBACK EDITION PUBLISHED IN 1992

Library of Congress Cataloging-in-Publication Data

Lerner-Robbins, Helene.
    Embrace change / Helene Lerner-Robbins.— 1st
HarperCollins paperback ed.
        p.   cm.—(Trusting intuition)
    "A Hazelden book"
    ISBN 0–06–255302–X (alk. paper)
    1. Twelve-step programs—Religious aspects—
Meditations.   2. Change (Psychology)—Case studies.
I. Title   II. Series: Lerner-Robbins, Helene. Trusting
intuition.

BL624.5.L47   1992b   91–58321
158'.1—dc20   CIP

92 93 94 95 96 K.P. 10 9 8 7 6 5 4 3 2 1

This edition is printed on acid-free paper that meets the American National Standards Institute Z39.48 Standard.

INTRODUCTION

Change is an undeniable constant in our lives. Whether we're facing problematical changes or getting ready to make positive changes, tapping into intuition is a practical means to handle these transitions. We need only get still enough and listen to its guidance. Over the past twenty years, I have found that one of the greatest gifts of recovery is that I have discovered my intuitive self.

Many changes have occurred in my life. And like most people, I fight change because it's uncomfortable to deal with new people and new situations. Yet I've discovered that by trusting my intuition, I no longer let my defenses dominate my actions. My heart's desire to expand and grow is stronger and dictates most of my actions now. When I have my off moments, they don't last as long as they used to. And I'm guided to reach out and get the support I need.

I've been fortunate to know many wonderful people over the years who have also transformed their lives. Their stories are shared in these meditations to offer you hope and courage to press on. You'll probably relate to many of their relationship and work issues and find their solutions applicable in your life.

These meditations are practical and can be used throughout your day. You can use the index at the back of the book to find appropriate topics. You can also use this book in the morning, starting your day with a few minutes of quiet time. Then open the book and see what meditation you're guided to. You will probably find that its theme is exactly what you need to focus on that day.

As you read this book, know that you have the power to *transform* your life. Open your heart as you speak the closing affirmation out loud. Say it three times. Each time, allow it to penetrate your being deeper and deeper.

Changing brings up many issues like risk taking, perfectionism, honest giving, and forgiveness. I've explored many issues that hold us back on our journeys, but I've also explored more comforting aspects of life that are always available to us as we continue to embrace change and tap into our intuitive resources.

I am open to all possibilities before me and know that only good can result from changing.

Old clothes, old friends, old habits, often feel more comfortable than new ones. That's why we hang on to them for so long, long past the time to give them up. Changing can be stressful and lonely when old ways don't work anymore. And there's a void that's left when we change, so the pull of the past remains strong. It can be centering to affirm at these times that "where I am right now is exactly where I'm supposed to be. I am enough, have enough, and do enough."

By accepting that transitions are painful, it's easier to struggle through them. I know a woman who recently divorced. She says, "During the separation, I suffered with the grief of a failed marriage and the fear of financial insecurity. I was depressed by the petty hassles of lawyers and accountants. At the same time, I realized I wasn't getting any younger, and I worried if I would find another mate.

1

"With a lot of support from friends I began to understand what went wrong in the marriage. I realized that I didn't stand up for myself and readily succumbed to my husband's demands. I resented him for *making* me do things, but it was really my fault. I never said no.

"Today I feel more special and complete than I did in the marriage. I had the courage to grow through the changes the divorce brought and was rewarded by increased self-esteem."

Help me respect the person I'm becoming.
Respecting myself as I am now will give me
courage to further change and grow.

I accept my past and see how it has shaped my life today.

When we go through painful times, we're often forced to get honest with ourselves and become receptive to change. Yet it's often difficult to view these situations in a positive way, that is, as a means for growth.

The experiences that challenge us the most are perhaps our greatest gifts: the job that we were fired from helped launch a new career; a divorce that created many sleepless nights led us to develop our spirituality; the acknowledgment of our weaknesses brought us to greater self-acceptance.

Growing through pain refines our character. And we can share our transformation with others, offering hope as they go through challenging times.

Help me regard pain as a catalyst for my growth.

I expect new good in my life and welcome it when it comes.

Why do we hold on to the pain of the past instead of moving on and experiencing new growth? There's safety in rehashing old traumas that have defined who we are for so long. Changing our perspectives and how we live can feel awkward and uncomfortable.

Like new clothing, changing feels stiff when we first try it. One woman who just lost fifty pounds commented on how awkward she felt wearing a sexy new dress, a dress she had fantasized about wearing for years.

She says, "I couldn't believe it was my body when I looked in the mirror. I felt like hiding. I've always wanted men to notice me, but I wished I had my old tank dress on. The more I put myself out there in this new way, though, the easier it got. Slowly, I began to enjoy the attention of people around me."

Stepping out in new ways becomes easier the more we do it. And as we begin to do it more and more, we experience a real joy for living.

Today I am grateful for the good You have put into my life.

I trust higher guidance to lead me in the direction of where I need to be.

Sometimes when we're ready to make changes, signs along the way point us in directions other than where we thought we should be going: a person we're attracted to is never there when we call; the paperwork for buying a potential residence we want gets lost; we get closed out of a seminar about a career we thought we should be moving toward. When we receive several red lights about something we want, it's time to reevaluate our goals. There may be some higher guidance at work suggesting we travel another path.

A charming woman I know says that when she's in doubt of whether to change directions, she asks God for a "big sign, a big arrow." "I don't need a little one," she says. "With me, I get too confused. I need God to make it big. And he does! I recently was looking for a different type of job in my company. I wasn't happy where I was and knew it was time to make a move. So I interviewed for jobs in different departments. Nothing happened, not even one potential offer.

"My husband suggested that maybe it was the company that was the problem. I took his advice and started to contact different types of corporations that excited me. Would you believe I got five interviews for different companies in one week? I guess God was giving me a big sign."

By seeing the signposts along the way, it is possible to change gears and take a new path.

Help me to be open to how You want me to proceed.

I embrace change and accept it as a necessary part of my growth and expansion.

When I first started my recovery program, I was feeling quite desperate. New emotions were coming up, and I was filled with fear. I had no idea of who I was. The old ways weren't working, and there was nothing to replace them with. One evening at a meeting I met this old-timer who told me that he could help me feel more peaceful. I wasn't in the habit of trusting anyone, but there was something in his soft blue eyes that told me it was okay.

Little did I know that our encounter would change my life. We went to an all-night diner and talked for hours. I felt totally safe expressing my fears and my pain. I cried like a baby. His eyes were so loving. He didn't say anything as I talked, but he seemed to know me better than I knew myself. For several hours I poured my heart out to him. And then I stopped out of pure exhaustion. I felt awkward because I wasn't sure what would happen next.

As if he sensed what I was thinking, he began to talk. The calmness of his voice mesmerized me.

"Close your eyes and picture yourself standing on a beautiful beach facing the ocean," he said. "Do you have the power to hold back the force of the wave coming toward you?" I looked at him skeptically, trying to understand his point. "There's something, Helene, that powers the universe, a force much greater than you and me." Up until that point, my spiritual background led me down one path—that of a nonbeliever. And now this wonderful man who I had no real reason to trust was suggesting that I accept something I had rebelled against all my life.

His intensity and conviction never waned as he continued to speak. "You can choose at this very moment to let go of your fear and embrace life. Give up the struggle."

"But . . ." came from my lips.

He lovingly interrupted me. "Buts make simple truths complicated." He then said emphatically, "You can choose to embrace change rather than fight it." Miraculously, a calm came over me. And that night, I gave up the struggle.

I'm not alone and can face anything with the help of my Higher Power.

Right now I have the ability to see the larger picture in all situations before me.

It's easy to get caught up in the petty occurrences of the day: a loved one speaking in a harsh tone, a child making his twentieth demand of the hour, a friend overlooking a special invitation. When these things come up (and they always do), we have a choice. We can either become irritated by them, or we can let them go and move on.

Detaching from these types of disturbances isn't easy. And many of us react angrily out of habit. Often, we are not aware of the toll these outbursts take on ourselves, our families, and our friends. But it is possible to change this behavior. One useful tool to use when we are bothered in this way is to ask ourselves, *How important is the incident when compared to my real priorities? Isn't it more important to have satisfying relationships with my family and friends than to dwell on minor irritations?* When situations are seen in this context, we can relax. And we realize that pursuing minor grievances will not bring us closer to our loved ones.

A couple describes how they've grown beyond fighting with each other. She says, "I was so upset about a comment my husband made to my parents. Later that night I told him how I felt. He heard me. I knew he didn't understand. But the fact that he heard was enough."

He recalls, "I listened to my wife and didn't agree with her at all. However, we kept the peace by *agreeing* to *disagree!*"

By quieting minor disturbances we win major battles. And by looking at the larger picture of our true priorities, we can watch hurtful grievances dissipate.

Help me to walk through this day by keeping the larger picture in mind.

*I allow myself to prosper
by experiencing completion in all my affairs.*

How many projects do we start but never complete? Do we take on too much at one time, thwarting success? Going the full measure means breaking with the past. When we do that, we own our power and leave behind the victim role. And we stop feeling guilty about surpassing the accomplishments of our parents or families. We are set free to *have* what we want in our lives.

Most of us yearn for relatively simple things: to express ourselves creatively, to feel a common bond with people, to give our love and be loved in return.

We deserve to experience these heartfelt desires. And we are capable of bringing them into our lives.

*Lord, help me understand that Your will for me is
to realize my full potential.*

*I have the resources to handle
whatever happens in my life.*

Sometimes life feels overwhelming—situations change, relationships fall apart, and we wonder, *How will I get through it?* Indulging in these thoughts has a negative, spiraling effect. And if we indulge them often, we can become debilitated.

How can we break this cycle when it starts? By recalling this simple principle: *We're never given more than we can handle.* A recovering alcoholic talked about how he has overcome situations that he previously would have considered crises.

He says, "Each day, I pray to know God's will and accept it. Sometimes it's rough when things don't go my way. Recently, I wanted my wife and kids to come back and live with me, but it didn't work out. That was really hard to accept. Today I have people in my life who I can share my pain with. And that's what gets me through difficult times."

When life gets tough, help me turn to supportive people around me to get me through.

> *Today I make loving choices for myself
> and accept good into my life.*

Making inappropriate choices usually comes
from low self-esteem and believing that we
don't deserve the best for ourselves. Believing
that we deserve less than the best is a spiritual
lie, because it's our birthright to live a prosperous life.

Louise Hay uses a wonderful metaphor to
show how we limit the abundance that is
available to us: If we go to the ocean to get
water, what size bucket do we take? Is it small,
large—how big is it? There's no limit to the
amount of water we can take, but we may
impose constraints on ourselves because of our
pasts, which keep us thinking small.

It's possible to replace old habits with new,
self-esteem-building actions. And one way to
do this is to act as if we deserve the best for
ourselves.

16

Eventually, if we keep it up, old habits will lose their grip as new actions will take hold, and we'll believe we do deserve the best.

Help me know that I deserve to make loving choices for myself throughout this day.

*I am committed to my growth
and prosperity today.*

Many of us look for commitment from others
so that we can feel secure. And we try to get
our partners or spouses to reaffirm how much
we are cared for. Looking outside ourselves this
way never works. Because even if we get what
we want today, there's always tomorrow, or
next week, or next month. The need for someone else to approve of us is *insatiable*.

Commitment starts with believing in ourselves. A friend of mine recently realized this,
and it created a profound transformation in
her life. She says, "I'd been dating someone
new who seemed to be very interested in me.
So I was surprised and disappointed when he
didn't call for a week, but this gave me time to
reflect on my patterns in relationships.

"I'd always been looking for a man to com-
mit to me. And, of course, I dated men who
were afraid of commitment, very much like my
father was. What I realize now is that I don't
need their commitment. What I need is to

make a commitment to myself: I am committed to taking care of me."

There's power in making a commitment to ourselves. Giving our word to doing everything we can to bring it about makes it happen.

Help me take a stand and hold on to the integrity of my commitments.

*I grow rich in my ability to compromise
and let other people into my life.*

Sometimes when we face change, we become inflexible, and we don't want to give up anything. Living without compromise is like living in a cage, where situations are safe and predictable. However, life becomes very isolated and lonely.

Compromise breaks down walls and enables us to get closer to each other. We give up our loneliness and feel connected to people. Compromise does not mean doing away with all of our boundaries, however. On the contrary, in order to compromise we must take stock of ourselves, becoming aware of what to hold on to and what to give away.

Why is it so hard to compromise? Because we give up control in situations that are not easily predictable. But the payoff is great because life becomes rich and expansive. We experience for the first time what it's like to be intimate with other people. In giving up our

20

separateness and becoming one among many, we don't lose our individuality but rather gain a better understanding of ourselves.

Lord, help me let go of my isolation so that
I can feel connected to other people.

*I am committed to taking actions that will
move my projects along today.*

It helps to view the projects we are working on
as divinely inspired. If we have this perspective,
we don't get caught up in the many voices of
our egos, which only keep us afraid and thinking
small.

When we are motivated by a greater purpose,
our jobs take on new meanings. We experience a
commitment to go forward, realizing our visions.
And we receive the strength and enthusiasm to
do it.

A friend described the difference between
approaching life from a place of fear and a place
of faith: "I own a service-oriented business.
Like so many business owners, I can get frantic
when I start thinking that similar businesses
are folding up and that the competition is

fierce. I find myself too paralyzed to do business. But when I remember that I have something people need that will make their lives easier, I take actions that bring new clients in."

Help me remember that God is my employer and my skills are his gifts to me.

☀ Forgiveness ☀

> *I forgive those who hurt me
> because they are in pain.*

Have you ever looked into the eyes of someone who's verbally attacking you? If you have,
you've probably recognized his or her pain.
Often those who lash out are hurting and are
unable to release their guilt or anger in any
other way. They feel separate and disconnect-
ed from the people around them.

When we realize this truth, we can learn to
be more compassionate and forgiving toward
those who attack us. But don't be surprised if
when we act in this new way, we feel conflict:
the force of habit can pull us back to feeling
resentment and anger.

How can we overcome this tendency to go
backward? A friend shared with me a practice
that works for her. "When someone is acting
out, I envision a glass door around me. I imagine the negative energy of the other person
being absorbed by the glass. This frees me to
observe what's happening in a detached way."

24

Sometimes it's helpful to treat the "attacker" as if he or she were out of sorts, as if the person were ill. You'd have compassion for a sick person. If you know the person well, it's also helpful to think of a time he or she was happier and more fulfilled. In this way, we don't counterattack and react negatively to the person's anger, but instead send out positive energy that may have a calming effect.

Help me have compassion for those who try to hurt me, for they are truly suffering.

25

I experience the power of an outflowing heart when my thoughts and actions are other-directed.

When we face change and difficulties, it's easy to get trapped in self-centeredness. We get caught up in thinking about what we *have* accomplished or what we *haven't*, what we *should* have done in a given situation or what we *shouldn't* have done, or who's to *blame* for the latest slight. When we become too introspective, life seems very bleak, and we feel isolated from those around us. What really helps at these times is to look outside ourselves. Is there a person who needs help? A situation where we can be of service? A chore that needs to be done?

There's great power in reaching outward. When we do it, we feel a sense of usefulness and purpose; feelings of hopelessness and depression can't survive in this type of atmosphere. Mildred Mottahedeh, a philanthropist in her eighties, puts it this way: "If you're sitting in a dirty room, the thing to do is to get a broom and clean it up. And that's always been the way I worked: something needs to be done and you do it."

When the urge to pull inward strikes and you start to worry, get discouraged, or feel criticized, take a look on the brighter side—the outward side.

Let me experience the blessings that come from being of service to other people.

*I accept the guidance from my heart
and handle my affairs with honesty.*

How often have you told other people what
you thought they wanted to hear, lying not
only to them but to yourself? This people-
pleasing behavior feels so uncomfortable.
When we do it, there seems to be no boundary
between where we leave off and other people
begin. We focus on what they want us to say or
do, and we lose ourselves.

What a disservice to our friends, never letting them know who we really are. How can
we begin to change and let go of this facade?

A very wise woman says that she started by
taking a baby step in a new direction. "Just do
something a little different each day, like saying no to a friend. Or get honest with yourself.
Or tell the truth when someone asks for your
opinion." A tall order, yes, but not impossible

if we take just *one* action. Remember, the tortoise won the race by keeping a slow and steady pace.

Lord, help me to appreciate
that change happens in small ways.
Give me the courage to take a baby step
in Your direction today.

Perfectionism

*I am compassionate and loving
to myself in every way.*

When we're trying to make changes in our
lives, it is natural to make mistakes. But why
are we so hard on ourselves when we make
mistakes? We show compassion to friends and
counsel our loved ones when they make mistakes, but we don't give ourselves the same
courtesy.

Many of us have difficulty accepting the
"total package" of our being, especially when
our dark side surfaces. When we are critical or
uncompromising, we relentlessly tell ourselves
that we should have done better. But our
defects are as much a part of us as our
attributes. And the only way to diminish their
influence is to *embrace them*.

A woman I know treats herself with compassion when she starts to get upset with the
way she's behaving. She soothes the little girl
in her. "I ask her what's wrong, and she tells
me. And I let her know that I understand. At
the same time, I'm firm and won't let her act

out. Treating her this way usually quiets the disturbance."

Being perfectionistic with ourselves keeps us stuck. It may feel safe because it's all we know, but we don't move forward by rehashing our mistakes over and over again.

Help me let go of my perfectionism so that I can participate more in the excitement of life.

Setting Limits

*I accept my limitations and am willing
to receive help from those around me.*

Why do some of us take on more than we can
handle? Why do we try to control so many situations around us? Why are we unable to
accept our limitations? Many of us feel that
people will judge us as weak if we can't fulfill
their requests.

A business acquaintance of mine explained
where his need to be all things to all people
comes from. He says, "When I was younger, I
was pretty much on my own. And no one
taught me to set limits. So I felt if people
expected something from me, I *should* do it. As
I grew older, this pattern got worse until I realized that always having to run things was run-
ning people out of my life. I realized I didn't
want to be on my own anymore."

Thank God for our weaknesses. Being superhuman is not only draining but also very lonely. Admitting our limitations allows others to fill in the gaps and take over where we leave off.

Let me be humble enough to accept
what I can and cannot do.

*I am open to the intuitive messages
that come to me throughout the day.*

It's been said that Einstein used only 8 percent
of his brainpower. Can you imagine what hid-
den resources are available to us, what stored
energy we have yet to tap into?

There is a power that flows through us that
can't be learned and is always available for our
use. It often comes in the form of a hunch or a
feeling. And if we follow it, we have clarity
about a situation that can help any noble
cause move forward.

A friend of mine was leading a workshop at
a corporation. As she was getting ready to
leave her house for the seminar, something
inside her said, *Turn on the television,* which
she did. A local news anchor had just
announced personnel cuts at that corporation:
ten thousand employees were to lose their
jobs. This invaluable information helped her
prepare to meet the workshop participants.

These intuitive messages are always available to us if we get still enough to listen for them. Quieting our minds is an important discipline. It enables us to be guided by the truth and to be of service to others in times of stress.

Let me get still enough to listen for the intuitive messages that come from my Higher Power.

I allow the excitement of change to fill my life.

Many of us get caught in the fear and anxiety created by the changing events in our lives. Yet if we look beyond the fear, we find that there's excitement in doing things differently. Unfortunately, we often hold on to the fear rather than experiencing this excitement. We end up robbing ourselves of wonderful moments. Why do we do this? Because when we're afraid, we know our limits, and that feels safe. Excitement can be baffling and unpredictable.

A friend of mine recently moved into a new home. She experienced both terror and excitement in changing locations. She says, "For a few weeks before I signed the lease I felt terrified. Could I meet the payments, would my furniture fit the new space, was this house too big for me? As I began to move my things in, something shifted. I felt elated, really happy and excited."

It's easy to hide in our fears and never experience the joy attached to doing something new. As we let go, we receive renewed vitality and realize each day has the potential to become a wonderful adventure.

Let me see beyond my fear and live in the expectancy of leading a joyous, prosperous life.

I release the fear that keeps me from moving on.

Sometimes we hold on to situations for fear of what the future will bring. And if our current circumstance has some gratifying elements, we hang on even tighter. It becomes like a golden handcuff. How could we move on when something is *this* good? But thinking this way stunts our growth and keeps us stuck.

A woman I know had a prestigious job at a Fortune 500 company. She had been there for some time but had outgrown the work. She says, "I had a deep desire to do something more creative, but because I was making so much money, I felt tied to the position. How could anyone leave a secure position, especially in the midst of a recession? My fear told me that if the new business failed, I'd never find a job as good as the one I had. I was deeply conflicted: I felt confident and ready to try something new, but I was also terrified of losing everything if I risked my security."

38

She took about three years to finally make the move. She acknowledged her fear and took action despite it, affirming her faith in her creative side. Now she is an artist, loves working as one, and is making a fine living at it.

Help me to have faith in my next steps, even if what lies ahead seems unclear.

*I am filled with expectancy
as I reach out in new ways.*

When I was younger I took few risks. I was afraid to. I convinced myself that playing it safe was the right way. But deep down I knew that I was denying my heart's voice, which was prompting me to reach for more.

Eric Butterworth, a wonderful Unity minister, calls that inner urge to improve "divine discontent." Our need to expand is spiritually inspired.

I now listen to and respect my yearnings to move on. But I need support to try new things. And people I trust coach me to launch out in different directions. There are times I feel stuck, so I talk with people who are doing what I want to do and ask them how they got started. This helps me slowly build my courage to take risks and to find opportunity in divine discontent.

> *Grant me the willingness to reach out*
> *for support today so that I may be open*
> *to greater adventures before me.*

*Today, I look at the people in my life as if I'm
meeting them for the first time.*

When we are involved with colleagues,
friends, and loved ones for a long period of
time, we set up expectations about them that
tend to limit new possibilities for each relationship. We remember old hurts and disap-
pointments, the times when our trust had been
violated.

Our lives are always changing, and so are
the lives of these important others. So why is
it difficult for us to acknowledge that our relationships can change too? Our fear creates dis-
trust, telling us that the same patterns will
always happen in our relationships.

A friend of mine was constantly complain-
ing about his wife. He recalls, "We seemed to
press each other's buttons all too often.
Actually, it got so bad that we sought profes-
sional counseling. The therapist pointed out
that I had little faith in my wife's ability to
change, and my attitude created a self-fulfilling
prophecy.

"At the suggestion of the counselor, I decided to experiment and think more positively. Instead of believing that she wouldn't be responsive to me, I visualized her meeting a request of mine. And you know, on the next occasion when I asked for something, she willingly accommodated me."

As in the case of my friend, when we become positively expectant, circumstances in our lives can be transformed.

Lord, help me experience the people in my life in a fresh way by letting go of old hurts.

*I respect the power of words
in creating my reality.*

Our words—the way we label people, places, and things—shape our reality. If we are constantly finding fault with those close to us, they feel criticized and insecure. If we are loving and supportive, they feel safe and confident.

Words are also an indication of how we really feel. To truly know our feelings, we need only listen to what we say. And when we do this, we can choose to alter our speech, changing our perspective. If we are angry or distressed by another person and need to release our feelings, it is better to say "I" statements rather than say "you" statements, which blame the other person. We can say, "I feel uncomfortable when you do this." Or, "When this situation happens, I feel anxious." By talking from our own experience, we open up the channel to better communication with others.

44

As a teacher, I experienced the power of words. One of my colleagues complained constantly about his discipline problems. A substitute teacher wouldn't dare volunteer to take his class when he was absent. His group was unruly and showed little respect for others. Another staff member had only the nicest things to share about her students. And her students reacted in kind. They were a most enthusiastic group to work with.

Help me realize the power of my words.
Help me use them to improve the quality of my life
and the lives of those around me.

Self-focusing

Today I am responsible for taking good care of myself.

It's so easy to get distracted, attending to everything and everybody around us, avoiding what we need to do for ourselves. Are we paying the proper attention to our health, our need for recreation and relaxation? Or are we becoming human "doings," getting caught in frenzied activities so that we don't do what we need to do for ourselves?

We deserve to treat ourselves well. And we can't really serve others well unless we do.

Let me remember
to act kindly toward myself
during this day.

Letting Go

*I release ideas of what is right
and trust my instincts.*

Many of us think that if we read the right books, attend the right schools, surround ourselves with the right people, we'll be happy. We seek contentment in all the wrong places. Using our intuition will lead us to another place. And like Dorothy in the Wizard of Oz, we'll find that home—our inner peace—comes from within.

Much of the time the ego part of our minds puts us on the defensive and is a *liar*. This simple realization is so profound. The ego can belittle, discourage, and destroy our inner peace. And one insidious thought begets another. In contrast, the heart knows instinctively what is right. It trusts and loves. *The challenge is to get still enough to listen to it.*

We have a choice whether to listen to our heads or our hearts. But it's often difficult to choose the latter when we're dealing with loved ones. A friend recently experienced this conflict when her husband lashed out at her in front of her twelve-month-old daughter. Her mind had a heyday with the incident. She thought, *You can't stay married to him, what about your daughter? She's learning to throw tantrums from her father. And how much abuse do you have to take?*

For days she held on to this pain. But in between the anguish, her heart was sounding another message, *Henry has been under a lot of stress lately, have compassion. He really tries to do his best for the family.*

She didn't pay much attention to this voice and chose to focus on the hurt. But the impulses from the core of her being didn't quit and sounded again, this time louder than before, *Forgive him, don't you lose it sometimes?* Still stubborn, it didn't register.

Finally, at her most desperate moment, she turned to God for help, asking, "How do I let go?" And the answer came. Instinctively, she knew it was time to speak with the little girl inside her who was making all the fuss. So she closed her eyes and imagined that she was walking with and talking to herself as a child of ten:

Adult: "I know you were hurt by Henry. It wasn't right for him to yell like that. And even if he doesn't realize it, we know it. I'm here for you, I love you, and I think you're terrific."

Child: "Mommy," her teary blue eyes looking up at her, "I love you so much."

They hugged. And the war inside her was over.

Help me be still and listen to my heart.

*I open up myself to an inner guidance
that counsels the truth in every situation.*

I used to think that by developing my intellect I would become serene and confident. So I pursued philosophy in college, reading all the right books and attending lots of lectures that talked about the meaning of life.

But much of this investigation proved futile in the end. I could "talk the talk," but I hadn't the slightest idea how to apply these doctrines to my life, especially when I faced changes. Now I'm learning to trust my heart, my inner guidance. Trusting our inner guidance may go against everything that made sense to us early on, but with experience we can come to believe that the heart never lies. And we can begin to rely more and more on our intuitive sense of people, places, and things.

A friend shared that even as a teenager he was aware of his intuition, but because of his people-pleasing behavior, he didn't follow it. He says, "My older sister was always daring me to do dangerous things against my better judgment. I really looked up to her so I did them. One night she dropped me off in a local park that was known to be unsafe at night and dared me to walk around. I was terrified but started walking. A person came up in back of me and asked for my money. I ran as fast as I could and was able to get away from him. That experience had a profound influence on me. I've learned *not* to go against my gut reactions. Today if I'm uncomfortable or frightened about something, it's because I should be."

Our intuition is linked to a divine guidance that is available in all situations. The problem lies with us when we don't get still enough to listen to it.

Grant me the willingness to listen
to the messages of my heart
and take actions based on its counsel.

Resentments

*I let go of resentments that keep me away
from my greater good.*

Many of us revel in our resentments and get a
charge from reliving them over and over again.
But by holding on like this, we lose valuable
energy to do positive things. And we block
greater good from coming into our lives.

When we begin to let go of this negativity,
situations materialize that we previously
thought couldn't happen, as was the case with
a friend of mine. A resentment had been fes-
tering in him for two years. It had to do with a
work colleague who had advanced, while he
had not. They had been close friends, debating
heavily on issues, meeting at conferences, and
enjoying the intellectual stimulation of being
together.

Although he wanted to let go of his anger,
he couldn't. Holding on became so painful
that he started praying to God for the willingness to let it go. During the next few months
he began to remember the good times his colleague and he had shared together, and he

started to grieve over the loss of his special friend. To his amazement his anger began to dissipate, and he was left with only warm feelings for his friend. It was as if his resentment had been exorcised.

About this time, this same colleague called him from out of the blue. He was amazed. Not only did they resume the friendship, but his friend hired him for a project that launched his writing career.

> *Lord, help me let go of old wounds and welcome the good in my life.*

I open my heart to the abundance around me.

Sometimes we forget how much the people in our lives affirm us. It's easy to get caught up with trivial things and lose the intimacy of the moment. When we're two steps ahead of ourselves, we become vulnerable to feeling empty.

The other night one of my closest friends paid me a compliment. "It's a privilege seeing you grow, Helene," Evelyn said lovingly. To my surprise, she stuttered as she spoke. My tall, self-sufficient friend, a woman who I looked up to, seemed vulnerable expressing her warmth. I felt both awkward and wonderful hearing her words. In the past I might have run from the closeness we had exchanged. But I didn't and hugged her instead. I'm learning to slow down.

What we all hunger for is love and a connection to others, but sometimes it's difficult to stay still enough to accept these things. Abundance is not just achieving material success or even stopping to smell the flowers. It also happens when we have the courage to say thank you and smile back at those who express their care for us.

With God's help, may I continue to open my heart to the abundance around me.

Divinity

*Today I experience myself and others
as children of God.*

Life becomes more serene when we can see the
divinity in people around us. It's useful to
believe that a Higher Power has created us and
that we all resemble this force. Unity minister
Eric Butterworth reminds us to greet everyone
we meet in this way: "The divinity in me
salutes the divinity in you." When we approach
challenging situations with this in mind, we
improve our lives and the lives of others.

Peter, a sales manager for a large corporation, was having a difficult time with his num-
ber-one sales performer, Howard, who had
been coming in late to work and not getting
his sales reports in on time. Peter talked with
him about this, but Howard kept doing the
same destructive things. Peter was about to put
Howard on probation, when a business friend
suggested that he have another talk with
Howard away from the office. "Treat him with
compassion," he counseled. "After all, he has
been your top salesperson for five years."

Peter took his advice and invited Howard to breakfast at a local hotel. "I told Howard how much I valued him as a worker and asked if everything was okay at home. I found out that his wife had been recently diagnosed with cancer. Howard felt bad about not getting his reports in on time but was finding it hard to concentrate on anything. I suggested that he take a few weeks off, which he agreed to do."

As Peter learned, when we pull back from potential upsets and look at these challenges from a spiritual perspective, we are more likely to experience the divinity in ourselves and in those around us.

*Help me not to react out of habit
but to see the spiritual side of any situation.*

*Today I am able to listen to my intuition
and articulate it.*

Many of us are learning to rely on our intuition and use it to guide our actions. However, knowing what's needed in a given situation is different from being able to *communicate* the information appropriately. Patrick, a friend of mine, recently shared how he's learning to put language to what he intuitively knows is true.

He says, "Teasing is considered very normal in my family, but I've never really liked being teased. One day, during a rare visit to my brother, I was watching my sister tease my niece. My sister was relentless. I looked at my niece Samantha and said, 'Samantha, just tell her to stop.' My sister started yelling at me, 'Don't you tell her what to do!' I thought, *How can I word this right?* It didn't matter that my sister was attacking me. That wasn't what was going on in my head. I was thinking, *How can I say this differently so that it's understood?*

"Later that week it occurred to me that all I would have had to ask was, 'Hey, Samantha, do you like being teased?' and Samantha would have said no. That might have stopped my sister's badgering without provoking any further disturbance. Putting the right language to my intuition is a big struggle for me. I've never had the language to communicate what I am feeling."

Like Patrick, knowing the right thing to do is just a first step toward *effectively* doing it. But we can, with the help of friends and our Higher Power, find the tools to communicate what's needed in any situation.

Help me get across to others
the intuitive truths that I know.

*Today I have the ability
to say no when it's appropriate.*

Saying no to others and not people pleasing takes courage, but the payoff is great: we gain increased self-respect. Getting honest about what we truly want is not as hard as we might think. What is more difficult is following through and acting on what we believe. If we fear that we may lose a relationship by telling the truth, then there wasn't much to the relationship in the first place.

Dorothy, a colleague of mine, was a champion people pleaser, always saying yes when she wanted to say no. During a self-esteem workshop, she dealt with this issue.

She says, "On Sunday it was my turn to do an exercise. Each person in the room was to ask me for something—anything. It was suggested that I look inward and respond to each request. At first a woman shouted, 'Give me your purse!' 'No!' I said. Next, a handsome man who sat next to me whispered, 'I want you to kiss me.' I was flattered and I did. 'Give

60

me a stick of gum,' the leader demanded. 'Sure,' I agreed, and gave it to him. Then a young man put his arms around me saying, 'Take off your blouse.' Angrily, I pushed him away and said, 'No way.'

"It was an interesting afternoon, to put it mildly. After that exercise I was able to answer exactly as I wished at nearly every opportunity with the group. Those few minutes of responding from my deepest, truest feelings started me on a track that I cannot turn back from. For a few minutes that afternoon I had a very real sense of being myself. I wanted more of it."

Like Dorothy, being true to our inner selves starts by taking small steps, and as we act in new ways, it becomes increasingly easier to get honest with ourselves and others.

Let me respond to people truthfully and not just tell them what I think they want to hear.

Today I acknowledge my fear, but go beyond it.

Behind any defect of character—whether it is anger, jealousy, envy, greed—is fear. We are either afraid of losing what we *have* or not getting what we *want!* We're terrified of losing or not getting a job, promotion, spouse, money. The list is endless.

When I was younger, I was *always* filled with fear. I gravitated toward a serene, older woman named Birdie. I called her my "sweet bird of youth." Each night before I went to sleep we talked on the telephone. Her message was always spiritually based, and I'd feel reassured after speaking with her. She used to help me focus on facing problems in the here and now. "Do you have enough money for *today?*" "Yes, Birdie," I'd say. "Well, then, that's all you need to concern yourself with." I'd hear her voice and a peace would come over me, because I was learning she was right.

One night after we had spoken for some time, I was again stricken with fears that I couldn't seem to shake, so I called Birdie back.

She told me to hold a mirror up to my face and look in it. "See what your fear looks like," she said. I saw frown lines on my forehead and my eyes were teary. "Now look beyond. See the warmth coming from your eyes." "What do you mean?" I challenged. "Just keep looking," affirmed Birdie.

Suddenly, I felt a tenderness come over me. I felt compassion for the face in the mirror. "Now, Helene, say to that face, 'I love you just the way you are.' And give yourself a big hug for me." What a wonderful woman Birdie was. She died about ten years later. But her loving spirit has never left me.

Help me to see my fear
for what it is—a smoke screen for Your love.

*I "act as if" in all my affairs,
and it becomes my reality.*

The past has left damaging scars on many of us. As a result, we sometimes approach new opportunities in self-defeating ways. "Acting as if" enables us to embrace our vulnerable side and not let it hold us back.

Old-timers tell newcomers about acting as if when they first come into Twelve Step programs. "Everything you think you can't do, you can if you act as if you can," says the old-timer. "No, I can't be rigorously honest with people," says the newcomer. "Act as if you can," responds the old-timer. "I'm too afraid to try for a promotion," says the newcomer. "Act as if you're not!" says the old-timer.

"I'm terrified of getting to know the wonderful man who just came into my life. He seems to be there for me, unlike the men in my past relationships, but I know I'll sabotage it!" says the newcomer. The old-timer urges, "Trust your heart; act as if you deserve a good relationship."

Acting as if means acting your way into right thinking, acting your way into right actions, not letting your low self-esteem dictate your actions. By acting as if you already have what you truly want, you're allowing good things to manifest in your life.

Grant me the willingness to act as if
I'm prosperous, joyous, and free.

*I listen to an inner guidance
and set appropriate boundaries with people.*

Many of us give for all the wrong reasons: to please others or because we think we "have to." And when it's time to make tough changes in our lives, we get terrified of setting our terms and holding to them.

A friend of mine found out the hard way that "no" needs to mean NO.

He says, "I always seem to say, 'No, but . . .' And it's the *but* that gets me into trouble. For example, in business, I never turn down clients. I know I shouldn't take some jobs because I'll never make a profit. But I rationalize that I'll need the money for cash flow purposes, or that I'll do them a favor. And when I take on the work, I resent these clients."

Holding on to resentments eats away at our inner core. So we need to stay firm and say no when we mean no.

Help me have the courage
to set my terms and hold to them.

*Today I accept people coming in
and going out of my life.*

Like the motion of waves rolling back and
forth in the ocean, people come and go in our
lives. Many of us find it difficult to accept it
when colleagues, friends, and loved ones
change and sometimes leave us. Instead of letting go and wishing them well, we may try to
manipulate them into staying a bit longer—
but this never works.

When we view their moving on as a natural
part of the ebb and flow of life, we're more apt
to accept a change in our own lives. While
there's a void that's left when we let go of people, we can make room for someone or something new to come into our lives. In this way
we can be positively expectant of our future
even during times of loss.

*Help me remember during changing times
that I'm whole and complete on my own.*

*Today I let go of painful experiences
and understand what purpose they serve
in my growth process.*

Unfortunately, many of us don't learn the lessons we need to learn until the pain becomes so great that we are forced onto our knees in desperation. That was the case for a friend of mine. Pamela put most of her energy into moving up the corporate ladder, and she did so quickly. Her business success was extremely important to her. She was raised by overly critical parents; nothing she ever did was right. All the more reason to relish her career.

She says, "When under pressure to meet a deadline, I would push my workers unreasonably. And because of my abrupt manner, I had a difficult time getting along with them. Of course, my staff finally rebelled and went over my head to my boss, who then called me in for a talk. I felt humiliated and defensive about what had happened. My boss felt that the problem was mine and suggested that I take a management course that would help me deal more effectively with employees. I reluctantly did so a few days later. But I still couldn't let go of the anger about how I had been *wronged*.

"I exhausted myself with worry. It was becoming more difficult for me to show up for work because I was furious with the employees who had humiliated me. I belong to a Twelve Step recovery group and was able to get feedback from the members. They asked me to focus on what I did to make my staff rebel. But I resisted their suggestions and matters got worse. I began calling in sick all the time. My anger was poisoning me. One morning, just before I was about to leave for the office, I got down on my hands and knees and pleaded to God for help.

"That day I was unusually quiet at work. Later on that evening I called a support buddy. 'Where did you go wrong, Pamela?' she asked. We talked for a good two hours. Together we were able to look at my insecurity and how inadequate I felt on the job. We talked about my fears and inability to take criticism because of my childhood experiences. During the next few weeks I noticed a significant difference in my attitude toward my co-workers. I was no longer angry and was able to see how I had been unreasonable."

Why is pain our greatest teacher? Because when circumstances become bad enough, we're forced to change.

Help me to see my part in creating
the painful situations in my life.

This is the day I begin a difficult task.

There's power in taking a first step and committing ourselves to go for something we desire. By doing this, we build up momentum to take other actions that will ultimately lead us to our goal.

Gregory recently declared that he was ready to sell his business and look for a new career. He says, "I finally got the courage after five years to get out of my business. I had to. It was taking too much from me. I was working a sixty-hour workweek and had developed ulcers. It just wasn't worth the money I was making.

"I saved enough money to keep me going for a few years, and it was time to make the move. When I let people know that I was interested in selling my company, several things began to happen. I got a few offers from prospective buyers. One person even wanted me to stay on to run it. No way! A friend suggested that I go to a career seminar, which I did. It's exciting to explore the many fields I could go into."

When we take small steps in a new direction, it doesn't seem so frightening. We can build on the momentum set by each previous action until we reach our final destination.

Help me walk through my fear by taking a small action toward achieving my goal.

*I receive from my senses and experience
the intimacy of the moment.*

How often in the day are we absorbed in our thoughts? *Almost always!*

We're often either thinking about a past problem or something that hasn't happened yet. We often live in either extreme and hardly ever in *the moment*. Why does this happen so much, especially when we see time and time again that this type of introspection leads nowhere? The answer is simple: it's a habit, and habits are hard to break.

But we can break through old patterns by using our senses. If we *see* or *touch* what's in front of us, *hear* the sounds around, *smell* the odors, and *taste* whatever is there, we find the key to living in the present.

Next time you find your mind wandering, *stop*, *look*, and *listen* to what's all around you. You'll be brought back to the vitality of the moment.

Help me live in the moment,
where life is truly vital and exciting.

Pressures

*Today I have enough time to take care
of what I need to do.*

Often we get caught up in the rush of an activity, feeling as if there's never enough time to do what we have to. Thinking this way only creates greater frenzy and a self-fulfilling prophecy. We end up not having enough time.

It's useful to stop whatever we're doing when a never-enough-time-attack comes on. If we then stop, tune into the sounds around, and appreciate our surroundings, we are brought back to a serene place. We can then reassure ourselves that there is enough time to accomplish important tasks.

A friend finds it useful to prioritize her activities. She says, "I write down all the tasks I need to take care of that day in the morning and then group them according to importance: Has to get done today; Can wait till tomorrow; Not that important. This helps me lighten my load and focus on what's essential."

There's always enough time to do what we need to do. What doesn't get done can usually wait until tomorrow. Everything happens in God's time frame anyway, so what's the use of worrying?

Help me rest in the stillness
when I get caught in time crunches.

*Today I accept that although our outsides
are different, our insides are the same.*

Many of us have developed a habit of comparing ourselves to other people. We go from thinking that we are uniquely superior to thinking we are uniquely inferior, sometimes from one minute to the next. When we do this, we block ourselves from feeling joyful and instead remain separate and alone.

What we are forgetting is a simple truth that we knew as children: our instinct is to *embrace* others, not separate from them. Just think of how a child relates to the world—almost always in a trusting, playful way.

Unfortunately, as we grow up, this joyfulness gets covered up. We develop personalities that are pleasing rather than truthful, we dress a certain way to maintain a certain image. We focus so much on measuring up that we forget what our real beauty is—the spontaneity and loving impulses we had as a child.

Help me be true to my real self
and experience the joy I once knew.

I am open to the opportunities
You place before me.

We are often aware of what we need but don't go after it because of obstacles in our way. If we listen to our inner voice, it will tell us how to break through these barriers. Consider my friend Carol, who knew she needed a vacation but couldn' tget herself to take one. "I can't leave work. My boss is in Japan for the next six months. Who'd run the office?"

Carol was responsible to a fault. She would go into the office at seven and leave at eight. She'd stay twice as long as she needed to, triple-checking her work and the projects of people she supervised. Her fastidiousness was a cover-up for her feelings of inadequacy.

One night she called me to complain about how stressed she felt. "I need a vacation, and I need it now. All I can think about is a Caribbean beach." But Carol couldn't get herself to take action to make it happen.

A few weeks later a high school chum invited her to go on a cruise. He had been one of the salespeople at his company and had won a vacation for two. He would be leaving in a week and needed an answer by the next day. Carol's response to him was, "I'd love to, but I can't get away. My boss isn't around, and I'm in charge." She called me later that night and told me about her invitation.

"Carol," I said, "this is what you've been asking for, and now the universe is giving it to you. Accept it."

I manage it, Helene?" she asked.

"Who's second in command in the office?" I questioned. "Tomorrow, give her a list of things that she needs to handle for the week while you're gone."

"What if something happens while I'm away? How will I explain it to my boss?" she timidly responded.

"You'll handle that when the time comes," I said. "Carol, do it. It's what you need. You said so yourself."

"Okay," she said with a little trepidation. "It's not like me, but I'll go."

Carol went on the cruise and had a wonderful time. As you probably guessed, there was no crisis at the office. Like Carol, we too can become accepting of opportunities presented to us. And as we do this more and more, we learn to take better care of ourselves.

Help me accept the gifts that
You put in my life today.

INDEX